Insights of Testing Machine Learning Models: A QA Perspective

Verses Kindler Publication

Verses Kindler Publication.

Website: www.verseskindlerpublication.com

Insights of Testing Machine Learning Models: A QA Perspective

By: Mr. Rahul Shetty (Venkatesh)

ISBN: 978-93-49532-20-5

FICTION STORIES 1st Edition

Price: INR 299/$15

Disclaimer

Insights of Testing Machine Learning Models: A QA Perspective is written by Mr. Rahul Shetty (Venkatesh).

The published work is the original contents of the author and he has done his best to edit and make it plagiarism-free.

The characters may be fictitious or based on real events but they are not meant to hurt anyone's feelings nor portray anything against any caste or system. Any resemblance of names of actual person, place or institute is purely coincidental to carry forward the story.

In case of any plagiarized write-up, the author is solely responsible for it, the publisher would not be responsible for it.

Table of Contents

Chapter 1 Rahul Shetty (Venkatesh) Learning Experience on Quality Assurance and AI Testing

Entering the world of QA, I discovered that although this position was in high demand, the job itself was unexpectedly straightforward in its requirements and execution. Software development has been booming, and then QA is its partner not to be missed. We wrote code, and we checked the requirements against the written code—no bugs, no surprises. We looked for defined cases, testing software on strictly defined checklists and checking for issues that occurred there. It was all system-based, logic-driven, and often predictable.

I couldn't have foreseen the rapid, almost unbelievable changes QA would undergo, mirroring the relentless pace of technological advancement. What had taken me years to transition from traditional software testing to the cutting-edge world of AI and ML model testing was suddenly condensed into a single, pivotal event that fundamentally reshaped my understanding of quality assurance. The shift was profound, impacting my perception of what QA truly entails.

This is how I came to navigate that transition from testing static systems to working with dynamic, always-learning AI and how that's affected my view of our future.

From QA to AI Testing

The move into AI testing was not so much a career goal, but a response to an increasingly changing landscape. My fifteen years in QA had shown me a consistent trend: companies are increasingly integrating AI, and the subtle yet significant shifts in software design were noticeable in every project. At first, it started with simple enhancements: recommendation engines, basic chatbots, or predictive analytics. As AI capabilities increased, so did the complexity of the systems they were expecting us to test.

One such experience was when I had the opportunity to work on an AI-driven fraud detection system of a financial services client. With the help of its ML model, the system scanned transactions, detecting anomalies and instantly flagging potentially fraudulent activity.

Unlike the traditional software, which made use of some pretty strict rules, the foundation of this model lies in pattern and probability. It might flag a transaction as suspicious based on some very subtle correlations in the data—things no human would ever notice.

Testing the system was very challenging. *How do you test a model that doesn't give you the same output for the same input? How do you know if the predictions are correct?* These questions made me think twice about my entire approach. The traditional testing method, reliant on fixed inputs and expected outputs, proved wholly insufficient. We needed new strategies that considered the probabilistic nature of the ML models and the complexities of their data.

The deeper my involvement in AI testing became, the clearer it became that the field was in its infancy. Few QA professionals had experience with it, and fewer with a clear-cut framework on how to test ML models. This significant gap, though initially intimidating, offered the potential to significantly influence best practices in a rapidly changing domain.

Important Experiences and Anecdotes

There are several experiences that came out from that journey, each teaching me really valuable lessons about the nuances of AI testing.

The Biased Data Challenge

My favorite project is an AI-based hiring platform. It screened resumes with some form of ML to rank candidates based on how likely they would be to succeed in a given role. A very great idea on paper: save time and avoid human bias in hiring.

But when we started testing the system, disturbing patterns emerged. The model always ranked male candidates higher than female candidates, even if their qualifications were identical. The development team was baffled at first. The model wasn't programmed to favor men; what was causing the bias?

In comprehensive tests and analyses, we found the problem was in the data that was provided. It was historical hiring data that the client had already worked with, reflecting actual existing biases in their practices about whom to hire. Essentially, the model learned it through biased data and began reflecting those biases.

The experiment not only showed whether these AI systems were correct or workable but also ethical in nature. It became clear that AI testing requires addressing both the technical aspects and the crucial ethical dimension of creating just and impartial systems.

Importance of Explainability in the importance of AI testing.

Another significant moment was working on an AI-driven diagnostic tool for healthcare. The tool, based on an ML model, analyzed medical images and presented potential diseases. During the testing phase, we faced an issue that recurred: the doctors were unwilling to accept the predictions of the model without knowing how the model derived its conclusions.

This exposed me to the concept of explainable AI (XAI). Traditionally, QA has always focused on whether the system works, but AI testing often asks us to explain why it works—or fails. For the diagnostic tool, we needed to develop techniques to trace the model's decision-making process and to communicate this in a way that was understandable to medical professionals.

This experience brought forth a more general truth about testing AI: AI systems have to be accurate but also interpretable and transparent. As QA professionals, we have a big role in ensuring this happens.

Handling the Unexpected Outcomes:

Probably the most challenging part of testing AI is the randomness of events. I remember one time testing an AI marketing tool that was generating product recommendations from customer data. Most of the time, it worked great, but in the middle of testing, it started suggesting children's toys to customers who didn't have children and had bought nothing like that before.

Through comprehensive analysis, we found that the cause was because of a quirk in the training data. The model had learned certain patterns of purchases correlating with the toy-buying behavior, but had overgeneralized in ways that the developers hadn't predicted.

This incident has been a lesson for all of us to realize the importance of robust testing scenarios. In AI systems, unexpected outcomes are not just bugs; they often tell a deeper story about issues that are part of the model design or data.

Book Purpose

Why am I writing this book? Because I believe that AI testing is one of the most exciting and challenging frontiers in technology — and one of the most misunderstood.

It usually goes too complex for old-school QA guys. Terms like "neural networks," "training data," and "model evaluation" are jargon enough and not to mention very daunting, especially for someone who has nothing to do with the background in data science. Let's proveLet's here and there prove to them that you don't need a background in data science to test AI.

This book is for the QA professional who wants to add something new to his repertoire, embracing the challenges of testing an AI system. It's for those who want to know not only how to test AI systems but also why they behave in certain ways. And it's for anyone who believes, as I do, that QA isn't only about finding bugs- it's about making sure the technology we build is trustworthy, ethical, and impactful.

This book will take you through practical strategies and real-world examples with actionable advice on how to navigate the AI testing world. Whether you're new to ML model testing or a seasoned expert looking to enhance your skills, I aim to provide you with the knowledge and resources you need to excel.

Vision for the Future of AI Testing

As I look ahead, I see AI testing as part of mainstream development. Historically, QA was always an afterthought at best, the final check before a product was released. But with AI, that needs to happen at every stage of development.

The biggest challenge that we face is the complexity of AI systems. The ML models that we use today are quite sophisticated, but it also becomes very challenging to understand and test them. It's here that I see QA evolving and we must look beyond just traditional testing methodologies. We need to come up with new frameworks that speak to the needs and challenges associated with AI.

For example, how would we test whether an AI system is fair? How would we ensure it was using accurate and unbiased data? How would we test if it is reliable in practice? These are just a few of the questions facing QA professionals in the future.

Explanation will become an increasingly vital factor in testing for AI in the future. Since AI systems, with greater autonomy, request more and more transparency, users will request to know not only what the system is doing but why. Essentially, QA professionals should cultivate new skills and tools to achieve this level of transparency.

In the future, I foresee QA professionals as core members of AI development teams, working alongside developers and data scientists right from the start of the software development project. To me, this is when we can expect such an AI system to be useful, ethical, reliable, and trustworthy.

In many ways, QA professionals can be referred to as guardians of quality in technology. It is a role that, in the age of AI, will be more important than ever. It's something I take seriously, and one that I hope inspires others.

That's all for the beginning of my adventure with AI testing. In the following chapters, I will discuss strategies, challenges, and opportunities in this exciting field. Let's together discover how to test AI systems, understand their complexities, and create value out of them for good. Let's get started.

Chapter 2 Introduction to Testing Machine Learning Models

I am only now moving deeper into this artificial intelligence world, and I have already found out that the complexity of the systems created by machine learning calls for an altogether new method to be used in testing. If a typical software test is primarily functionally and performance-based, then ML model testing challenges us to enter a world characterised by uncertainty, ever-changing dynamics, and an intricate interplay between data, algorithms, and real-world behaviour.

In this chapter, I'll unpack why ML model testing is so important, the unique challenges that arise, and how I have tried to shape my testing philosophy around it. By the end, I hope to give you a solid foundation for understanding the role of QA in AI applications and why it's so important to get it right.

Why Do We Need ML Model Testing?

Testing has always been considered one of the most fundamental processes involved in a software development cycle and, consequently, ensures that a system functions as desired. **However, ML models differ because there isn't an understanding of "working as desired"**.

ML models are not hard-coded with any rules; instead, they learn patterns and make predictions on the basis of data. This flexibility makes them extremely powerful but also unpredictable. Unlike conventional systems, where outputs are determinable, ML systems often result in probabilistic results, meaning their outputs can change with regard to the type of data they are fed. This variability makes rigorous testing not just important but essential.

Making Sure It's Reliable

It primarily aims to guarantee the reliability of an ML model. Consider the scenario of a health application utilising an ML model for identifying cancer from images received in medical setups. Such models, which performed efficiently in a controlled environment and failed in unpredictable real-time environments, would bring about havoc. Testing would ensure consistency in the behaviour of a model across various scenarios, from controlled environments to the unpredictable situations of real-time.

Creating Trust

Another significant factor is trust. The user must believe that what the model says it will do, that which will actually happen, is real and just and explainable to themselves and others. As such, a financial institution has an interest in making sure an ML loan approval model does not favor applicants of certain types. Testing and identifying such issues is good because they help build confidence.

Handling Change

The ML models adapt and evolve over time based on new data available. The risk introduced by this flexibility is model drift, which means that the performance of a given model degrades as its data pattern drifts. Such risks can be chased down with continuous testing, making sure the model stays effective.

In short, ML model testing isn't just about verifying functionality; it's about safeguarding the integrity, fairness, and trustworthiness of AI systems.

ML Testing Challenges

Testing ML models isn't easy. Over the years, I've encountered several recurring challenges, each requiring a unique approach to overcome.

- **Data Dependency**

Data is the lifeline of an ML model, and the quality dictates the performance of the model. As opposed to traditional software, where the code is central, ML models are highly dependent on data used to train them. Poorly quality data—either incomplete, biased, or irrelevant—may result in a false prediction.

For instance, I had a machine learning model that was meant to predict customer churn for a subscription-based service. During testing, we noticed a consistent overestimation of churn rates for one specific demographic group. After further investigation, it was found that the training data for this particular demographic group was sparse and skewed. In this case, the model draws wrong conclusions from those distorted data. That means it is necessary to test the data pipeline and the model.

- **Model Drift**

Model drift happens when the performance of a model deteriorates over time because of the changes in the data that the model encounters. For example, an ML model trained on consumer behaviour data from five years ago may find it difficult to make correct predictions today because consumer preferences have changed.

One of the memorable projects is testing a recommendation engine for an e-commerce platform. Initially, the model did very well, suggesting relevant products based on users' browsing history. However, with time, as the platform introduced new product categories, the model's performance started declining. Regular testing and retraining were necessary to keep the model relevant.

- **Interpretability**

Another significant challenge is interpretability. Many ML models, especially complex ones like deep neural networks, are black boxes. They produce results without providing insights into how those results were reached.

This lack of transparency can be an issue in applications where explainability is the core requirement. For instance, in a legal tech project I was involved with, the ML model predicted case outcomes. Lawyers were required to understand the reasons for which the model was making its predictions to effectively use the system. Testing for interpretability led to the need for developing tools and techniques that could extract meaningful explanations from the outputs of the model.

- **Ethical Issues**

Perhaps the most difficult issue for ML testing is ethical concerns, especially bias and fairness. That is, biased models can both perpetuate and exacerbate biased data, leading to unfairness.

One of the most striking examples came from a hiring recommendations project involving an ML model. As I mentioned in the previous chapter, the model showed gender bias due to biased training data. Such issues require not only rigorous testing but also a deep commitment to ethical principles.

Rahul's Applied Testing Philosophy

Over time, I've developed a results-oriented philosophy for ML model testing, one that focuses on real-world applications and industry relevance. My approach is grounded in three key principles: **context**, **adaptability**, and **collaboration**.

Context is Everything

One of the first lessons I learned is that testing doesn't happen in a vacuum. Every ML model operates within a specific context, and understanding that context is crucial. For example, the testing strategy for a healthcare diagnostic model will be very different from that for a social media recommendation engine.

In my work, I always start by asking: **What problem is the model trying to solve?** Who will use it, and under what conditions? In that way, by knowing the purpose of the model and its constraints, I am in a position to design tests not only thorough but relevant for real-world use cases.

Adaptability is key

ML systems are by nature dynamic, and my testing approach is the same. Traditionally, QA relies on predefined test cases, but with ML, those cases often need to evolve in tandem with the model. For instance, when testing a fraud detection model, I keep updating test scenarios to fit new types of fraud emerging in the market.

Adaptability also deals with the acceptance of new tools and techniques. I am always looking for innovative avenues to make testing more potent, from the use of synthetic data for simulating edge cases to the exploration of explainable AI frameworks.

Collaboration is success

Testing an ML model is a team effort-it involves not just QA experts but also data scientists and developers, domain experts alike. The best results will come from a collaborative setup where everyone puts in their specific expertise.

For example, while testing a model for predicting equipment failures in manufacturing, I collaborated closely with engineers who knew the machinery and its failure modes. Their insights were invaluable in designing realistic test scenarios and interpreting the model's predictions.

A Pragmatic Approach

My philosophy, at its core, is pragmatic. Testing, I believe, should be results-oriented and more concerned with real-world performance than theoretical perfection. An ML model may pass all lab tests but fail in the field if the testing does not account for real-world complexities.

For example, once, I worked on a model that was supposed to analyse sentiments on a social media platform. Controlled tests were very good, with an almost perfect identification of positive, negative, and neutral sentiments. However, once deployed, it didn't do well with sarcasm and slang, where it had not been trained very well. By incorporating real user data into our test cycle, we were able to address these shortcomings and make the model more accurate.

The Road Ahead

Testing ML models is as much an art as a science. It requires some technical know-how, critical thinking, and creative problem-solving. But above all, it requires a commitment to quality and a willingness to embrace complexity.

As we move on in this book, I will give you a better understanding of the practicalities of ML testing-from designing good test cases to dealing with specific issues such as bias and interpretability. I hope that you will be able to learn all the tools and mindsets that will help you shine in this exciting field.

The journey of ML testing is just beginning, and the possibilities are endless. Let's explore them together.

Chapter 3: Understanding the ML Model Lifecycle and QA Scope

Machine Learning (ML) has transformed the design and testing of software systems. Traditionally, the code tells you what happens; the ML model learns from the data and changes according to what it discovers. This natural ability of the ML model renders the lifecycle complex and makes the testing rather unique. In this chapter, we'll be looking at the lifecycle of the ML model, testing objectives at each stage, and differences between ML model testing and traditional software testing.

Phases of the Machine Learning Lifecycle

The ML model lifecycle is an iterative process with several connected stages. Each phase is crucial for developing a reliable, high-performance, and scalable ML system. Understanding these phases clarifies the QA scope and ensures systematic validation at every step.

1. Data Collection

Data is the blood of a machine learning model. Gathering data that is relevant and representative of the whole is the first activity in the ML lifecycle that may be sourced through databases, web scraping, IoT devices, APIs, and user-generated content.

Barriers to Data Collection:

- The data could be incomplete and noisy.

- It is difficult to collect representative real-world data.
- Laws and ethics regarding data privacy and security.

Testing Objectives:

- **Relevance of Data:** The QA team must ensure that the data obtained is relevant to the problem that the model tries to solve.
- **Diversity of Data:** The dataset must present different scenarios so as not to introduce bias to the model.
- **Volume of Data:** Ensure that the volume of data is enough to train without overloading the computational resources.

For example, if a product review sentiment analysis model is developed, the QA team should make sure that the data set used has reviews from more than one region, various languages, and different types of products.

2. Data Preprocessing

Raw data is hardly clean or structured. Data preprocessing is cleaning, transforming, and organising data into a format suitable for training an ML model. This step includes removing outliers, handling missing values, normalising features, and encoding categorical variables.

Challenges in Data Preprocessing:

- Ensuring the cleaning process doesn't remove important data patterns.
- Normalising features without distorting their significance.
- Addressing imbalanced datasets where certain classes dominate others.

Testing Objectives:

- **Data Quality:** The QA teams would have to check that the cleaned data was free of inconsistencies, duplicates, and errors.
- **Feature Engineering validation:** Verify that the engineered features are relevant and improve the learning by the model.
- **Class Distribution:** Check and balance class representation that skewed prediction results.

For example, in fraud detection, preprocessing should handle the class imbalance because fraudulent transactions occur much less than legitimate transactions. QA can use any of the techniques like Oversampling or Undersampling to build balanced datasets and test their accuracy.

3. Model Training

In the training phase, patterns are learned from the preprocessed data by ML algorithms. This phase includes the right algorithm selection, hyperparameter tuning, and optimization of a model for performance metrics like accuracy, precision, recall, or F1 score.

Challenges during Model Training:

- Selection of the right algorithm from the many that are available, such as a decision tree, neural network, and SVM.
- Overfitting, where the model tries to memorise the training data and not generalise the patterns.
- Ensuring that the hyperparameter tuning does not introduce bias or degrade performance.

Testing Objectives:

- **Convergence Checks:** Ensure that the model is training well and achieving the desired performance metrics.
- **Overfitting and Underfitting Tests:** QA teams must check whether the model is generalising well or just memorising the training data.
- **Reproducibility:** Check that the training runs produce consistent results given the same conditions.

A classic example of overfitting is that of image recognition models. The model performs well on training images but fails on new ones. QA must implement techniques like cross-validation and regularisation to mitigate such risks.

4. Model Validation

This is an important validation phase that makes sure the model is good on unseen data. In this phase, a separate validation dataset is used to evaluate the accuracy of the model, its ability to generalize, and robustness to variations in data.

Challenges in Model Validation

- The validation dataset does not represent real-world scenarios.
- The performance metrics may not be able to capture the subtleties of the task (for example, false positives vs. false negatives).
- Over-optimization by the model during hyperparameter tuning can lead to model drift.

Testing Objectives:

- **Validation Metrics:** QA should test the model against the metrics that are relevant to the business objective, for example, precision, recall, or mean squared error.
- **Bias and Fairness:** Ensure that the model's predictions are not biased against any particular groups or attributes.
- **Robustness Checks:** Check how the model behaves with noisy, adversarial, or incomplete inputs.

For example, in medical diagnosis models, QA should ensure fairness so that the model does not underperform for specific demographic groups, ensuring equity in healthcare delivery.

5. Deployment

Deployment is where the validated model gets integrated into production environments from which it begins to give real-time predictions or makes real-time decisions. Therefore, this step usually requires pretty close cooperation with software developers as well as operations teams ensuring that the deployment goes smoothly.

Challenges in Deployment:

- Compatibility with existing systems and APIs.
- Performance under High loads or distributed systems
- Handling edge cases or unexpected input

Testing Objectives:

- **Integration Testing:** It is required to ensure the model's seamless operation within the broader application architecture, encompassing API interactions and data pipelines.
- **Latency and Throughput:** Check if the model would be capable of meeting performance requirements for real-time predictions

- **Error Handling:** Check how the model would perform if exposed to out-of-distribution or corrupted data.

For example, in an e-commerce recommendation system, QA should test the model to ensure it integrates well with the website's backend and provides relevant recommendations with minimal latency.

6. Maintenance

After deployment, the ML model needs to be regularly monitored and updated for continuous good performance. This phase takes care of model drift or concept drift that changes data distribution over time which causes its accuracy to deteriorate.

Problems during Maintenance

- Model drift or concept drift detection and correction.
- When to retrain the model, and what data to include
- Tradeoffs of retraining with how important it is to be precise.

Testing Objectives:

- **Performance Monitoring:** Monitor key performance indicators like accuracy, latency, and failure rates in field deployment.
- **Data Drift Detection:** Identify drifts in the underlying distribution of the data affecting the model's performance.
- **Retraining Pipelines:** Check whether the retraining workflows are efficient and perform consistently over time.

For instance, in fraud detection systems, as fraudsters evolve their tactics, the model needs to be retrained on updated data to stay effective. QA teams play a vital role in validating the updated model before redeployment.

Testing Objectives Across the ML Lifecycle

There are several overarching testing objectives throughout the lifecycle that guide the QA process:

- **Quality Input Data:** Because ML models are data-driven, the quality of input data is proportional to the quality of the model built. QA teams should focus on validation, cleaning, and transformation of data so that it is rugged at the foundation.

- **Avoiding overfitting and underfitting:** Overfitting occurs when the model learns too well about the training data but fails to generalise. Underfitting takes place when the model is very simple and cannot capture the underlying patterns. QA plays a very significant role in identifying and preventing these issues through techniques like cross-validation and parameter tuning.

- **Post-Deployment Monitoring and Updating:** QA does not end with deployment. Continuous monitoring has to be done to catch drifts, biases, or performance degradation in the models.

ML vs. Traditional Software Testing

Testing ML models is very different from testing traditional software. Here are a few key differences and implications for QA professionals:

1. Deterministic vs. Probabilistic Outputs

- Traditional software produces deterministic outputs—given specific inputs, predictable outputs can be expected.
- On the other hand, the ML models give out probabilistic answers based on learned patterns. QA must test an extensive range of acceptable results while keeping track of levels of confidence.

2. Quality of Data

- Traditionally, the correctness of the underlying logic behind the code is in focus
- Here, in ML, what governs the behavior of a model is the quality of data. Poor quality data results in bias, low prediction accuracies, and ethical concerns.

3. Self-evolving Systems

- Traditionally, software does not change unless it is updated.
- ML models evolve over time and have to be retrained, re-validated, and constantly monitored. QA has to ensure that updates do not break existing functionality.

4. Ethical Issues

- ML testing involves aspects like fairness, explainability, and accountability, which do not apply in the traditional testing. The QA professionals need to be aware of these ethical concerns.

5. Testing Metrics

- Traditional software is tested against predefined functional and performance requirements.
- In ML, testing is primarily based on metrics such as precision, recall, F1 score, and AUC-ROC, along with qualitative measures like interpretability and fairness.

Understanding the scope of QA at each phase in the ML model lifecycle will form the basis for dependable AI systems. While the traditional software is deterministic and not data-driven, this type of system is dynamic and probabilistic, hence challenging conventional ways of testing. Validation of input data to monitoring post-deployment performance, QA professionals provide significant value in delivering safe and responsible AI solutions.

By adopting a systematic, phase-wise approach to testing, QA teams can ensure that ML models not only meet performance expectations but also align with broader societal values, paving the way for a future where AI is both powerful and responsible.

Chapter 4: Early Testing Strategies in ML Engineering

Such practice, known as Early (shift-left) testing, now proves quite instrumental, most especially in Machine Learning, adding to the importance of Software Development and Quality Assurance, as the name suggests- "shifting" its testing activities to the preceding part of the development lifecycle with the aim of reducing its cost of fixing errors that may have occurred, better in terms of model robustness, and collaboration between all data scientists, developers, as well as QA professionals.

This chapter will explain why shift-left testing is critical in AI/ML projects, what actionable strategies one can do to ensure quality and mitigate the overfitting/underfitting, and put these into practical cases by taking an experience from me.

Why Early Testing Matters in AI/ML?

It takes place much later within the lifecycle of traditional software testing, pretty much at or near implementation time. That is likely to create a large number of issues when deployed with Machine Learning models. The ML models are data intensive, dynamic, and probabilistic in nature. When errors or biases creep in at the data acquisition stage or during data preprocessing, or even while designing a model, they tend to cascade all through the entire lifecycle to become increasingly difficult to identify at a later stage and more costly as well.

Challenges in AI/ML Testing

- **Data-Driven Behavior:** The behavior of machine learning models is determined by their underlying data. Poor-quality data impacts the performance of the model.
- **Iterative Development:** The ML model is continuously trained and retrained with new data. Testing at each stage is critical to maintain reliability.
- **Ethical Concerns:** Issues such as bias, fairness, and transparency need to be addressed early on to avoid building an unethical or unreliable system.

Benefits of Shift-Left Testing in ML

- **Cost Efficiency:** Industry studies have shown that correction of any defect identified in early periods costs between 5 and 10 times lesser in a production line.
- **Robustness of Model:** By early testing, models are created based on clean, representative data and better-validated architectures.

Shift-Left Testing allows involving QA teams early. Thus, such testing encourages good communication among teams so that all the confusion and inefficiencies are avoided. In myl's words,

"When working on ML projects, it's not enough to wait till the model is trained to begin testing. By then, the damage is done. Instead, shift-left testing can allow us to build quality into the system from very early on."

Testing Data Quality: Accuracy, Relevance, and Lack of Bias in Data

Data is the backbone of any ML project. Model performance is directly related to the quality of data with which it is trained. In terms of shift-left testing, one of the core principles is ensuring data quality early on in the life cycle.

Steps to Ensure Data Quality

1. Data Accuracy

Data accuracy refers to the correctness of the information collected. Errors in data—such as typos, incorrect labels, or duplicated records—can significantly skew model performance.

Testing Activities:

- Automate duplicate and inconsistent entry detection.
- Applying statistical tests for detecting outliers and anomalies.
- Checking data against known standards or benchmark sources.

Example:

In a sales forecasting model, poor sales records may be 10 times more than the real sales values. Early accuracy checks prevent this kind of mistake from propagating.

2. Data Relevance

Not all data is useful for the problem being solved. If noisy or irrelevant features are also included, then the model gets confused and its generalization capability degrades.

Testing Activities:

- Conduct EDA to find out irrelevant or redundant features.
- Validate that the data represents the domain of interest. For example, if one were building a model to predict weather, ensure that the dataset contained relevant climatic variables.

Example:

For example, in developing a recommendation system for a streaming service, if including customer billing addresses in the dataset that are irrelevant may cause the model to overcomplicate unnecessarily.

3. Bias Detection

Bias in the data will result in models that might discriminate against particular groups or not generalise properly.

Testing Activities:

- Check for Imbalances in the dataset. Does one class dominate others?
- Tools like Fairlearn or Aequitas can identify possible biases.
- Reduce bias by resampling, reweighting classes, or by generating synthetic data.

Case study:

I recall that I had a hiring model project based on historical data that was biased against women. Early bias detection made it possible to rebalance the dataset, and fairer predictions were ensured.

Data Quality Testing Tools

- Great Expectations: A framework for validating and document data pipelines.
- Pandas Profiling: Generates in-depth report on the data set, pointing out potential areas of issues.
- DataCleaner: Automatically cleans and preprocesses raw data.

My Insight:

"Data quality issues are the silent killers of ML projects. If you do not test for data quality early, no amount of fine-tuning later will save the model."

Understanding Training Data, Test Data, Overfitting & Underfitting—A Beginner-Friendly Guide

When learning **Machine Learning (ML)** for the first time, it's essential to understand how models learn from data. Before we talk about complex terms like **Overfitting and Underfitting**, let's start with the basics.

---

1 What is Training Data & Test Data?

Machine Learning models are like students preparing for an exam.

- 📚 **Training Data** → This is like the study material a student uses to prepare. The model learns patterns from this dataset.

- ✍️ **Test Data** → This is like a final exam. The model has never seen these questions before, and we check how well it performs.

Example: Predicting House Prices 🏠

Let's say we want to build an ML model that predicts house prices based on features like **size, location, and number of bedrooms**.

Size (sq ft)	Bedrooms	Location Score	Price ($)
1000	2	8	250,000
1500	3	9	350,000
2000	4	7	400,000

- **Training Data** → The model learns from this data, finding relationships between size, location, and price.

- **Test Data** → An additional set of houses the model has never seen before. It predicts prices and we compare them to actual values.

Now, let's see what can go wrong while training our model.

---

2 What is Overfitting? (Too Much Learning) 📈

Overfitting happens when a model **memorizes the training data instead of understanding general patterns**.

🔍 **Analogy:** Imagine a student who memorizes every question in the textbook but struggles when the exam has slightly different questions.

🔴 **Problem:**

- The model performs **extremely well on training data** but **poorly on test data** because it learned every detail instead of understanding general trends.

- It may even learn **irrelevant noise** (like an outlier in data) instead of the actual relationship.

📉 **Example:**

If our house price model was overfitting, it might assume:

"A house with exactly 3 bedrooms and 1500 sq ft will always be $350,000!"
Instead of learning a **general pattern** like: *"Larger houses in good locations cost more, but price varies slightly."*

☑ **How to Fix Overfitting?**

1. **Use More Training Data** → Helps the model see diverse examples.

2. **Regularization (L1/L2, Dropout)** → Prevents excessive complexity.

3. **Simplify the Model** → too many parameters can cause memorization.

---

3 What is Underfitting? (Too Little Learning) 📉

Underfitting happens when a model **is too simple and fails to learn important patterns** from the data.

🔍 **Analogy:** Imagine a student who only glances at the textbook and assumes, *"Every answer is 42."* They don't learn enough and fail the exam.

🛑 **Problem:**

- The model performs **poorly in both training and test data** because it hasn't captured key relationships in the dataset.

📉 **Example:**

If our house price model was underfitting, it might predict:

"All houses are priced at $300,000, regardless of size or location."

This happens when the model **cannot learn complex relationships**, like how location affects price.

☑ **How to Fix Underfitting?**

1. **Increase Model Complexity** → Add more layers (for deep learning) or use a better algorithm.

2. **Train for Longer** → More time learning improves performance.

3. **Feature Engineering** → Add relevant features (e.g., crime rate, school quality) to improve predictions.

---

4 \Finding the Balance: A Well-Fitted Model 🎯

A good machine learning model should **perform well on both training and test data**. It should learn **general patterns** but not memorize unnecessary details.

📌 **Key Takeaways:**

✓ **Overfitting** → Model memorizes training data, fails on new data.
✓ **Underfitting** → Model is too simple, fails to capture important patterns.
✓ **Ideal Model** → Learns general patterns and performs well on unseen data

Case Example: My Experience with Shift-Left Testing

The Challenge

One of my consulting team was supposed to come up with a predictive maintenance model for industrial equipment. This model was supposed to predict failures in machines based on the sensor data, which meant saving the client huge costs in downtime. Early issues threatened the project:

- The dataset had missing values and noise.
- The models generated initially provided high accuracy in the training set but a pretty poor validation result.
- Rework opportunities were severely limited by deployment deadlines.

How Early testing (Shift-Left) Approach helped here:

1. Data Quality Checks

In the data collection phase, the team carried out automated checks:

- Missing values have been imputed using both mean and median strategies.
- Noise in the readings of sensors has been smoothed using methods of moving averages.

2. Regularization and Cross-Validation

- To avoid overfitting, the team
  Applied L2 regularisation during training.
- Used 10-fold cross-validation to test the generalisation of the model on parts of the data

3. Collaboration Across Teams

- Having the QA team onboard earlier was helpful in throwing some of the data back at them for feedback of likely biases and holes in validations.

Results

- **30% Error Improvement:** Data quality testing so early ensured the catching of problem propagation that crept into training.
- **20% In Time-Saved: Cross** validation and use of early stopping result in some rework-saving during process optimization of hyper parameters.

- **Higher Reliability:** The final model behaved similarly with the validation and real data.

Early Testing the ML models is not a technical practice, but more of a mindset: making early intervention the prime issue for ML engineering. Indeed, addressing data quality, overfitting, and underfitting during the lifecycle's initial stages makes models much stronger, reliable, and ready to be deployed in the real world.

My experience highlights the true advantages of early (shift-left) testing: fewer errors, faster development cycles, and higher-quality ML systems. As the AI/ML field continues to advance, it will become essential for teams looking to deliver impactful and trustworthy solutions to embrace shift-left strategies.

Our development process prioritizes quality at every level, guaranteeing that performance targets are met while upholding ethical and operational standards; this will contribute to a future where AI strengthens industries and communities.

Chapter 5: Model Validation Testing-Core Strategies and Types

Validation testing is the final stage of the machine learning (ML) lifecycle. It is the last validation test before a model is deployed to a production environment, and its purpose is to ensure that the model behaves reliably, ethically, and efficiently across a broad spectrum of scenarios. While training models emphasise algorithms to learn from data, validation testing ensures that what is learned translates into something actionable and real-world in performance.

This chapter covers essential strategies and kinds of model validation testing that decompiles specific strategies such as cross-validation, hyperparameter optimisation, and edge-case testing. In the latter part of this chapter, we're going to talk about an in-depth case study in validating a conversational AI model like ChatGPT, wherein we will point out the application of strategies that may lead to ideal results. Lastly, common validation mistakes and how not to fall into them will be outlined.

Validation Testing Objectives

Before describing the methods, it is important to introduce a more general concept-the purposes of validation testing. Validation testing has one primary purpose: checking if model learning is to any extent useful in practice and, in its extreme interpretation, determining whether it's enough for a model to actually work under a wide variety of conditions and perform well, thus achieving its objectives in practice.

Primary Aims of Validation Testing

- **Generalisation:** Test the strength of the model in unseen data. A good model should avoid overfitting on training data and generalise effectively in new situations.
- **Robustness:** The model must behave reliably under different conditions, like noisy or incomplete inputs and unexpected user behaviors.
- **Fairness:** Validate that the model gives equitable outcomes and is not biased against particular groups or inputs.
- **Scalability:** Check if the model can work out heavy loads and scale without deterioration in performance.
- **Explainability:** Confirm that decisions derived from the model can explain to stakeholders why they made decisions, thus ensuring trust and accountability.

Validation testing finds out that a model may be accurate but also be of good use in reality, reliable, ethical, and scalable.

Specific Testing Types and Strategies - 25

The following are 25 critical types of validation testing and approaches used to ensure a thorough assessment of ML models. These techniques address a wide range of aspects of performance, reliability, fairness, and scalability.

1. Cross-validation and Hold-Out Testing

- Cross-Validation: In this method, the dataset is divided into k folds, and the model is trained on K-1 folds and tested on the remaining fold. This process is repeated for all folds.
- Hold-Out Testing: Sets aside a subset of the data (20% for example) and trains on the rest.

- Goal: Evaluate how general the model is to data it has not seen, and whether it overfits or underfits.

2. Hyperparameter Testing and Tuning

Before moving towards hyperparameter testing and tuning, let us first understand what hyperparameters are and their importance in machine learning.

Hyperparameters are the tunable parameters of a machine-learning model that govern how it learns from data. They are defined before training, whereas parameters such as weights or biases are learned by the model during training. In fact, they are learned only once during training. They determine how the learning process is to be controlled, and hence, they significantly impact the performance of the model.

- Grid Search: Brute force testing of all combinations of hyperparameters.
- Random Search: Randomly draw subsets of hyperparameters with the hope of faster optimisation.
- Goal: Optimize the hyperparameters of parameters like learning rate and the number of layers that improve the model performance.

3. Testing Accuracy, Precision, and Recall

- Accuracy: It is a measure of the overall correctness of predictions.

- Precision: This is the fraction of true positives among all positive predictions.
- Recall: It is the fraction of true positives identified among all actual positives.
- Goal: Balance these metrics based on the special use case, such as the medical application, which will then focus on recall.

4. Edge Case Testing

- Test how the model behaves upon unexpected or extreme inputs, such as in ambiguous queries or corrupted images.
- Goal: Whether the model responds to edge cases non-crashingly with reasonable outcomes.

5. Stress Test

- Load test the scenarios of thousands of concurrent requests or huge data volumes.
- Goal: Check whether your model functions and performs correctly under stress conditions or not.

6. Bias and Fairness Testing

- Apply Fairlearn or Aequitas libraries; conduct bias analysis on the outcome along with measurements of equitable outcome
- Goal: Detection of bias for the elimination of the unfair bias toward proper AI ethics.

7. Noise Robustness Test

- Random noise or distortions are applied to input data to test the model's performance.
- Goal: The model should still work well in real-world applications where data is likely to be noisy.

8. Outlier Detection

- Test the model on points that are drastically different from the ones it was trained on.
- Goal: The model should not make extreme or erratically erratic predictions when it encounters outliers.

9. Data Drift Testing

- Test the model on new distributions or scenarios than what it was trained on.
- Goal: Identify and correct performance degradation from data drift.

10. Interpretability Testing

- Apply tools such as SHAP or LIME to explain model predictions and ensure they make sense based on domain knowledge.
- Goal: Establish trust through interpretability of the model's decisions as sensible.

11. Sensitivity Analysis

- Examine how minor changes in input features affect predictions.

- Goal: Key characteristics and stability of predictability.

12. Monte Carlo Simulations

- Run the model on noisy data sets to test its stability and consistency over different scenarios.
- Objective: Test the robustness of the model.

13. Benchmarking

- Compare the performance of the model against known industry benchmarks or current best practices.
- Objective: Verify that the model is good enough or better than what is required.

14. Simulation of Real-World Scenarios

- Simulate real-world conditions, such as noisy inputs or shifting distributions of data.
- Objective: Check how the model is ready for deployment to its target environment.

15. Feature Importance Verification

- Verify the contribution of features to predictions by methods such as permutation importance.
- Goal: Confirm that the model correctly ranks the feature importances and ranks the top features in the right order.

16. Testing of Imbalanced Datasets

- Test how well a model performs on imbalanced class distributions

- Goal: Validate that the model does not bias towards dominant classes.

17. Adversarial Testing

- Give adversarial examples that can deceive the model.
- Goal: Determine weaknesses and enhance robustness to attacks.

18. Latency Testing

- Test how long it takes for the model to output under different loads.
- Goal: Make sure the model is compliant with latency standards, especially in real-time applications.

19. Model Calibration

- Determine whether predicted probabilities are consistent with the actual likelihoods.
- Goal: Enhance the usability of probabilistic outputs.

20. Class-Specific Validation

- Test the model for individual classes or categories.
- Objective: Find and solve class-wise accuracy or recall discrepancy.

21. Deployment Environment Testing

- Test the model in the production environment for APIs, databases, and other system compatibility.
- Goal: Avoid integration issues during deployment time.

22. Continuous Integration Testing

- Tests should be part of a CI/CD pipeline.
- Goal: Early catch of performance regressions.

23. Energy Efficiency Testing

- Quantify how much computational resources training and inference are consuming.
- Goal: Optimization of resources to save money and also to save the earth.

24. Retraining Validation

- Validates the model after having retrained with new data.
- Goal: Be relevant and reliable in the long term.

25. Ethical Testing

- Test the model against ethical requirements, such as privacy compliance and societal implications.
- Goal: Develop responsible and trustworthy AI systems.

Case Study: Model Validation for a Conversational AI

Project Overview

My team was tasked with the validation of a conversational AI model like ChatGPT. The model was supposed to generate responses that were contextually appropriate to the user queries. It had to balance the accuracy and reliability of responses with the ethical considerations involved.

Challenges

- The model failed on fuzzy queries and sensitive topics.
- Latency was more than acceptable limits during high concurrency.
- We found evidence of gender and demographic bias in the responses.

Validation Process

- Cross-validation: The training set was divided into ten folds for a consistent result across the subsets.
- Edge Case Testing: Inputs of slang, typos, and incomplete sentences were put to the test for robustness
- Bias Testing: Tools such as Fairlearn identified biases on sensitive topics, which were resolved by rebalancing the training data
- Latency Testing: The model was stress-tested with large volumes of queries to measure the response times.
- Explainability Testing: SHAP analysis revealed the key features influencing predictions, improving trust and transparency.

Results

- Error Reduction: Bias mitigation reduced inappropriate responses by 30%.
- Performance Improvement: Latency decreased by 20% after architectural optimisation.
- User Satisfaction: Positive feedback increased by 25% in post-deployment surveys.

Common Errors in Validation Testing

Despite its criticality, validation testing is vulnerable to common pitfalls that can affect the results. Some of the common pitfalls are:

- Not Testing Edge Cases: Not testing for corner cases may lead to a nasty failure.
- Overlooking Bias: Not testing for fairness and ethics may lead to biased predictions.
- Relying on Accuracy Alone: While accuracy is a metric that is important, metrics such as precision or recall should not be overlooked.
- Insufficient Scalability Testing: Not stress-testing the model may lead to performance bottlenecks in production.
- Neglecting Collaboration: Lack of communication between teams can cause missed opportunities for improvement.

Validation testing is a vital phase in the ML lifecycle, ensuring that models are accurate, reliable, and ethical before deployment. By employing diverse testing strategies—ranging from cross-validation to bias detection—teams can build robust AI systems capable of thriving in real-world conditions.

My case study exemplifies the tangible benefits of systematic validation testing: how edge cases, fairness, and latency challenges were addressed to deliver a high-performing conversational AI model. As the field of AI continues to grow, robust validation practices will remain crucial for building responsible and impactful technologies.

Chapter 6: Responsible AI Testing: Ethical, Fairness, and Privacy Testing

The invasion of AI in our daily lives has never been in greater demand than now for these systems to be fair, ethical, and privacy-compliant. Responsible AI testing refers to the evaluation of ML systems not just in terms of technical correctness, but also greater implications for society. Such a practice would ensure that such systems operated on and remained aligned within ethical frameworks, did not enable further harmful biases, and protected the user data. The approach is not just testing, but a multifaceted approach to fairness, bias, ethics, and privacy.

This chapter reviews the foundation aspects of responsible AI testing, approaches used in detecting and mitigating bias, approaches to data privacy and compliance, and an example illustrating my experiences as I used responsible testing techniques to get an AI system to a desirable ethical outcome.

Definition of Responsible AI Testing

Responsible AI testing is an all-inclusive test of AI systems wherein their outputs are in alignment with high ethical standards and also maintain privacy protection, while ensuring that fairness is maintained.

Responsible AI testing, unlike traditional performance testing, measures a much more profound implication for the model to be tested, its influence on an individual, a community, and an entire society.

Key Pillars of Responsible AI Testing

- **Fairness**

Fairness deals with ensuring that AI models give equal outcomes for various demographics and do not feature any kind of favoritism or discrimination. For example, an AI model used when hiring should take into consideration applicants regardless of gender, ethnicity, or socio-economic status.

- **Bias Detection and Mitigation**

Bias in AI systems may originate from imbalanced training data, inappropriate algorithms, or poorly chosen features. Responsible AI testing might reveal and rectify those biases in a way that the resulting model does not propagate societal prejudices.

- **Ethical Responsibility**

AI systems must be designed and tested for duty within ethical boundaries. This encompasses safe use cases, transparent decisions, and adherence to moral values.

- **Privacy Protection**

AI systems operate primarily with sensitive user data, so privacy protection is very critical for the organization. Responsible testing will ensure that the data remains anonymous and in a well-protected system and shall be used within the lines of GDPR and CCPA.

- **Government Rules Compliance**

There will be observance of local and international legal requirements so that these AI systems will remain accountable to the data they use. There will also be minimal bias, and there will be enough transparency.

My Insight -

"Responsible AI testing isn't just about preventing errors; it's about making sure that AI works for everybody, respects individual rights, and aligns with the values we hold as a society."

Example: Responsible Ethical Test Cases in Large Language Models

Consider one well-known LLM, ChatGPT, and illustrate the concept of responsible testing of AI. Let's take an example of the healthcare company's customer support chatbot being powered by that model. The model, when not responsibly tested, will make inappropriate, even harmful errors, like.

Hallucinated response: Such chatbots can fabricate medications or treatment plans, causing dangers to users' health. It could suggest the name of an imaginary drug meant to cure a medical condition and hence not only endanger life but also threaten to land the company with the courts for some legal liability.

Bias in Answers: If the model has been trained on biased data without ethical oversight, it might produce discriminatory answers. For example, giving priority to one demographic group over another when discussing healthcare access might be seen as prejudice and damage to the reputation of the company.

Misinformation: The chatbot may state confidently that a particular treatment is a "100% cure" when, in fact, no such guarantee exists. This can lead to misleading users and further tarnish the organisation's credibility.

Impact of Neglecting Ethical Responsibility

When responsible AI testing is skipped, the consequences can be severe:

Reputational Damage: Users would lose confidence in the healthcare company as they would view it as careless or unethical. Press regarding biased or dangerous AI could be negative, thus affecting the reputation of the company further.

Legal and Financial Risks: Ethical lapses could lead to lawsuits, regulatory fines, or even bans on using AI systems in certain regions.

User Harm: The most important impact is the harm on individuals—whether physical when giving bad medical advice, or emotional when giving offended or biased responses.

How Responsible AI Testing Prevents Harm

Ethical testing does this:

Safe Use Cases: The chatbot restricts responses to its scope and only gives recommendations to its users on how to seek more complex advice from professionals.

Bias Mitigation: Testing identifies and addresses biases in training data to ensure that the responses are fair and non-discriminatory.

Transparency: The model explains its limitations. For example, it can say, "I am an AI and not a licensed medical professional." This would be a way of controlling the expectations of the users.

Companies protect their users and reputations with these measures while ensuring that AI works as a tool for positive impact rather than harm.

Bias Detection and Correction

Bias in AI systems can be one of the harder problems to solve. It can take many forms but generally comes accidentally, and the outcome is extreme: discrimination or a suboptimal outcome for some groups.

Types of Bias in AI Systems

- **Data Bias**

Data Bias: The training dataset is skewed or not representative enough of the general population. For example, an object detection model trained to primarily only light-skinned faces could cause failure for the correct detection of darker-skinned people.

- **Algorithmic Bias**

This is mainly because of designing the algorithm. For example, an optimisation of model accuracy by majority class without attention given to the less dominant ones.

- **Measurement Bias**

Measurable bias occurs when data used is biased, either in terms of features or in labels. Therefore, if historical hiring data is discriminatory then, those hiring models will also be discriminatory.

Bias Detection Techniques

1. **Demographic Parity**

Compare two different models developed for two different groups with different demographics to treat both equally; for instance, an artificial intelligence-based credit scoring model will need to provide equal proportions of approvals towards women and men, assuming constant factors.

2. **Equal Opportunity Metrics**

Check whether the model is fairly accurate for all the subgroups. Therefore, an example of such a model that detects cancer can have balanced true positives amongst the subgroups.

3. Tools for Detection of Bias

- Ai Fairness 360: IB developed an open-source kit to identify and remove it.
- Fairlearn: It will check whether the model and improve it for fair discrimination.
- What-If Tool: Google's tool to check any model that will operate in all the data slices with different bias values.

Bias Correction Techniques

1. Data Balancing

Balance the training data set either by oversampling the underrepresented groups or downsampling the overrepresented ones.

2. Reweighting

Assign weights to data samples such that minority groups have equal influence during training.

3. Fairness-Aware Algorithms

Introduce fairness constraints into the objective function of the model so that it ensures fair outcomes.

4. Adversarial Training

Use adversarial networks to detect and correct biases during training.

Example:
I once worked on a healthcare AI model that predicted readmission rates for patients. Upon the initial test, the model was performing poorly for patients from rural areas, showing an imbalance in the dataset used for training. My team rebalanced the dataset and applied fairness-aware algorithms to enhance accuracy for all demographic groups.

Privacy Assurance: Data Privacy, Model Compliance and Regulation Compliance

Privacy assurance falls in responsible AI testing as it maintains the privacy of user data on which an AI depends to ensure compliance with law in place.

Major Privacy Issues that Exist in AI

1. Data De-Identification

User PII requires de-identification or masking, and hence, storage should have access control so that only authorized persons with access are permitted to manage and monitor data.

2. Data Storage and Access Control

Sensitive data should be placed in secure locations, and access controls have to be so restricted that no illegal usage is allowed.

3. Model Privacy

A model itself can compromise confidential information if an attack of model inversion or membership inference is initiated.

4. Regulatory Compliance

- AI models have to abide by the following privacy legislation:
    - GDPR: Provide provisions for gathering data based on user consent and a user's right to delete any information.

- CCPA: It is clear in its use of data and gives users the option to opt-out.

Privacy-Preserving Techniques

1. **Differential Privacy**

Differential privacy is that method where from the output produced by the model, it cannot identify a single data point. For example, differential privacy can keep a person's data safe, whereas the overall accuracy of the model is maintained by making a noise in the prediction done by the model.

2. **Data Minimization**

In this method, only as much information as the AI system requires is collected and processed, which therefore reduces the exposure extent to the minimum.

3. **Encryption**

Data encrypts both in transit and at rest to prevent access to data unless authorised.

4. **Access Testing**

Ensure only designated users or applications are entitled to rights on the sensitive data available.

Privacy Testing Techniques

1. **Data Anonymous Test**

All PII data is removed from the data set before input into a pipeline.

2. **Audit Trail**

Test to confirm all data access and usage are audited as necessary.

3. **Compliance Testing Validation**

Verify that the application meets the requirements of the GDPR, CCPA, and other laws and regulations.

Example Workflow:

Personalised Learning

- Anonymize Data: Student names should be replaced by pseudonyms.
- Encrypt Data: An encryption algorithm should be added to mask learner histories
- Compliance Testing: This system will allow data erasure requests from the student end, just as GDPR requires.

Case Study: Rahul's Road to Testable Responsible AI

Project Background

My team was building a path for an AI model based on an e-learning portal. One-to-one paths have been provided using grades, demography, and learning profile data while determining the learning path suggestions for a student.

Problems

- Algorithmic bias in the recommendation

The first testing had biases towards the students from urban schools and was blamed on the uneven training data.

- Privacy

The model used sensitive data about the students, thus raising issues regarding data protection and compliance.

Responsible AI Testing Process

1. Bias Detection and Mitigation

- Demographic Analysis: The team conducted a demographic analysis on the accuracy of the recommendation and found that the urban students were getting better recommendations.

- Bias Mitigation: The group ensured the fairness of results by providing samples of rural students within the dataset. Also, fairness-aware algorithms were used.

2. Privacy

- Anonymisation: The identifiers for the student were replaced using pseudonyms so that they would be masked.
- Differential Privacy: Techniques are applied such that no individual student's information could ever be derived from any one of the outputs of a model.

3. Ethical Governance

- The team consulted the educationist and parents on the ethics of the model and what educationists expected from this.
- Reports of transparency: It gives information about recommendations made to students and about addressing bias.

Results

- Privacy compliance: this system ensured adherence to all GDPR and CCPA regulations.
- The transparency reports and the ethical oversight instilled faith in the minds of educators, parents, and students.

My Reflection

"This project taught me that responsible AI testing isn't just about meeting technical requirements—it's about understanding the broader impact of AI and ensuring it works for everyone, not just a privileged few. "

Common Challenges in Responsible AI Testing

1. **Lack of Representative Data**

Using an unbalanced dataset may lead to biased outcomes.

2. Overfitting fairness constraints

Over-correcting for fairness can degrade model performance for the majority group.

3. Complex Regulatory Landscape

Multiple privacy regulations can be a challenge for global applications.

4. Transparency vs. Privacy

Transparency vs. privacy is difficult because more transparency exposes sensitive data.

This would denote responsible AI testing for fairness, ethics, and privacy compliance. Such testing for AI systems will remove all biases, ensure fairness to all, and protect privacies in developing societal values-compliant AI system development.

My case serves as an example illustrating that responsible AI testing is transformative in achieving ethical outcomes. As AI advances, practices such as these will make all the difference between engineering not only intelligent but just, fair, and trustable technologies.

Chapter 7: Continuous Monitoring and Maintenance for ML Models

Deploying an ML model into production is not the end of a project but the beginning of an iterative process of monitoring, evaluation, and maintenance. Unlike traditional software systems, the dynamics of ML models are sensitive to changes in data distributions, user interaction patterns, and other extrinsic factors. The need to monitor these models for constant effectiveness, reliability, and compliance over time calls for continuous monitoring.

This chapter delves into how one sets up continuous monitoring for ML models; it also highlights key metrics and alarms, the role of automation in monitoring, and comprehensive best practices to maintain continuous model performance.

Why Continuously Monitor?

Once the ML model is deployed in production, it operates within an uncertain real-world environment such that:

- Data drift has taken place because of shifts in input data over time, degrading model performance.
- Model Drift happens because of the evolving nature of real-world patterns, which makes the initial phase of training data irrelevant.
- Unknown Errors and anomalies like the sudden spike of prediction errors, latency or bad handling of edge cases

- It is important that proactive detection and remediation make sure the model is able to provide value throughout its lifecycle.

Configuring Continuous Monitoring

An effective monitoring framework is the base for keeping ML models. This framework includes tools, techniques, and processes needed to monitor model behaviour and react to deviations.

Key Steps to Set Up Continuous Monitoring

1. Define Monitoring Objectives

Monitoring begins with defining what one wants for model performance. Objectives depend on what business problem the model solves. For example:

A fraud detection model emphasises low false negatives to reduce missed fraudulent transactions.

A recommendation engine focuses on click-through rates (CTR) as a metric of user engagement.

2. Choose Metrics to Monitor

Metrics to monitor are:

KPIs.

Metrics to monitor should cover the following:

Model Performance: accuracy, precision, recall, F1 score, mean squared error, etc.

Operational Performance: Latency, throughput, error rates, resource utilisation.

Business Impact: Conversion rates, revenue impact, and customer satisfaction.

3. Design a Monitoring Pipeline

A monitoring pipeline will automatically collect, process, and analyse metrics in real time. A normal pipeline will have the following steps:

Data Collection: Input data, predictions, and system events are logged.

Data Analysis: Data processing for calculating metrics and detecting anomalies is performed.

Visualisation: Metrics presentation in dashboards for stakeholders.

Alerting: When metrics fall outside an acceptable range, teams will be notified.

4. Select Monitoring Tools

There are many tools that can assist with the setup and maintenance of monitoring systems:

Prometheus: Open-source system for collecting metrics in real-time, which can be monitored

Grafana: A visualisation platform that can create dashboards for monitored metrics

AI: Specially designed for ML performance and drift metrics tracking

Arize AI: This is a commercial ML observability with more complex features, such as root-cause analysis

5. Baselines and thresholds

This defines the expected performance at the model validation time. Example:

Latency: <200ms for real-time prediction

Accuracy: ≥85% on test data.

Drift: Less than 5% difference in distribution of data.

Metrics and Alerts

In order to track the performance of an ML model efficiently, you must determine appropriate key metrics that can illustrate how good and reliable your ML model is. Generally, metrics can be categorised into model-specific, operationally related, and business-related measures.

Model-Specific Key Metrics

- Accuracy: That describes the general correctness level of predictions.
- Precision and Recall: Highly relevant where class distributions are skewed, as in fraud detection scenarios.
- F1 Score: A metric that balances precision and recall for an overall performance measure.
- Drift Metrics: Monitor changes in the input data (data drift) and output predictions (prediction drift).

Let's use a **spam email filter** as an analogy to explain **precision** and **recall**. Imagine you've built an AI model to classify emails as either **spam** or **not spam**, and now you want to evaluate how well it performs using these metrics.

Definitions

- **Precision**: Out of all the emails predicted as spam by the model, how many were actually spam?
- **Recall**: Out of all the actual spam emails, how many were successfully identified by the model?

Scenario

You receive **100 emails**, and **40 of them are spam**. After running the emails through your filter:

- The model predicts **30 emails as spam**.
- Among these 30, **25 are actual spam**, and **5 are not spam (false positives)**.
- Out of the 40 actual spam emails, the model missed **15 (false negatives)**.

Operational Metrics

- Latency: the time taken by the model to give predictions. Critical for real-time systems.
- Throughput: The number of requests processed in one second. The higher, the more it is desirable and an absolute requirement for scaling.
- Error Rates: percentage of responses failed or wrong.

Business Metrics

- Conversion Rates: percent of users achieving your desired action, purchase click or conversion.
- Revenue Impact: How much revenue is being added to the organisation?

- Customer Retention: Measures of the ability of the model that trigger more user engagement

Set alerts for Anomalies

Alarms are alerts that are triggered when a monitored metric goes out of range from predefined thresholds. They allow teams to respond to potential issues quickly.

Steps to Configure Alarms

1. **Thresholds**

Thresholds can be defined using baseline metrics of acceptable ranges. For instance, if precision drops below 80%, trigger an alarm.

2. **Severity Levels**

Categorize alarms based on the severity of the alert. For example:

Critical: Prediction accuracy is 70% and below

Warning: Latency is beyond 200ms

3. **Real-time Alerts**

Alerts can be set up on stakeholders through email, SMS, Slack, etc.

4. **Predictive Alerts**

The machine model will predict anomalies based on past data trends.

For example:

My group used alarms to monitor the performance of a financial fraud detection model. Whenever it dropped below 85% and there was a sudden spiking in fraud patterns, an alarm automatically forced the system to retrain and this restored performance within hours.

Automation in Monitoring

Automation is required for managing the complexity of a monitoring and maintaining an ML model. Automation of repetitive tasks avoids inconsistency, human error, and allows teams to focus on high-value tasks.

Why Automation Matters?

- **Scalability**

Automated monitoring systems may work on multiple models concurrently, even in a high-load environment.

- **Proactive Maintenance**

Automation may track the problems at their origin often before they are communicated to the users.

- **Efficiency**

Saves time and resources consumed by human monitoring and interventions

Automated Monitoring Tools and Techniques

- **Automated Dashboards**

Grafana, for instance, may collect real-time data directly from monitoring systems and automatically render them on dynamic dashboards.

- **Drift Detection Tools**

Evidently, AI and Arize AI detect the data and prediction drift; the teams are notified of performance degradation.

- **Self-healing pipelines**

Configure the system for retraining or reverting to earlier versions of the model whenever a problem is encountered.

- **CI/CD Integration**

Integration in the Continuous Integration/Continuous Deployment pipeline will include auto tests on the model update, ensuring quality before deployment

- **Auto alerting**

Auto alert the teams with PagerDuty, where automatic escalations workflows can notify the correct people at the correct time.

Example Workflow:

My team automated their monitoring process by using Prometheus and Grafana:

- Prometheus tracked in real-time metrics like latency, accuracy, and drift
- Grafana visualized these metrics such that trends and anomalies are immediately discerned
- When drift reaches 10%, an auto script will start retraining on the new data

Continuous Monitoring Best Practices

- **Monitor Early**

Start monitoring at development, and testing levels to provide benchmarking and detect problems even before deployment

- **Holistic Monitoring**

Use metrics of the whole ML pipeline, not only of the model. Track steps, such as data preprocessing, feature engineering, and API performance.

- **Review Metrics Periodically**

Periodic checks help keep the thresholds applicable since business needs change with time.

- **Log Granularly**

Granular logs of the inputs, outputs, and error messages reduce the diagnosis time when faults occur

- **Involve teams**

Make data scientists, engineers, and business stakeholders aware of the monitoring to address the critical concerns of all business parties.

Practice Continuous Monitoring:

A Project Description

My team built a real-time recommendation engine for an online shopping portal. It processes user behaviour and transaction history to make recommendations of products tailored to the user.

Monitoring Challenges

- Data Drift: The input data distribution changed seasonally due to changing user preferences.
- Latency: Recommendations had to be delivered within 150 ms so that the user experience did not break.

- Scalability: During sales events, traffic increased dramatically, stressing the model and backend systems.

Monitoring Setup

1. **Metric Selection**

- Model Metrics: Precision, recall, click-through rate (CTR).
- Operational Metrics: Latency, throughput, server load.
- Business Metrics: Conversion rates, average order value (AOV).

2. **Tools Used**

- Prometheus for metric collection.
- Grafana for visualization.
- AI for drift detection.

3. **Automation**

- Automated drift detection caused retraining whenever input data was highly divergent from the training data.
- Load balancing systems automatically grant more resources during traffic peaks.

Results

- Improved Reliability

The continuous monitoring of models ensured that performance was stable and did not degrade during peak traffic periods.

- **Downtime Reduced**

Automated alerts ensured the team could address the problems within minutes, causing the least amount of disruptions.

- **More Revenue**

Continuous tracking of CTR and AOV helped optimize the recommendation engine that resulted in a 15% sales during peak events.

My Reflection

"Monitoring continuously transformed our recommendation system from a static model to a dynamic, adaptive solution. Automation was crucial in ensuring seamless scalability and top-notch performance.

Continuous monitoring and maintenance of ML models are key to successful performance in real-world environments. By defining key metrics, using automated tools, and establishing robust monitoring pipelines, teams can ensure that their models always remain reliable, scalable, and effective.

My experience with monitoring is a great example of how continuous monitoring can be useful for maintaining trust, delivering business value, and adapting to changing conditions. As AI evolves, these practices will be indispensable for ensuring that ML models deliver consistent and impactful results throughout their life cycles.

Chapter 9: RAG-Based LLMs and Evaluating Them Using the RAGAS Framework

Large Language Models (LLMs) have forever changed our interaction with artificial intelligence; they make applications of the likes of chatbots, summarisation, translation, and question answering possible, though as the models go increasingly large and complex; they become a big deal: hallucinations, domain specificity, and non-temporal and non-spatial updates are some of the current and daunting issues these face.

Retrieval-augmented generation (RAG) is a fast-rising hybrid approach that links LLM's generative strength to the retrieval system, ultimately presenting a more accurate and relevant in-context response. Chapter overview The mechanics of LLMs that are based on RAG are described while detailing its strengths and shortcomings in relation to its feasibility as well as presenting the RAGAS framework that is a robust model to systematically assess this feature.

What Are RAG-Based LLMs? A combination of two elements;

- **Retrieval**: Search for related data in external databases or datasets, including databases, knowledge bases, or even web resources.
- **Generation:** Answers are generated through a pre-trained language model, given both the user's question and the retrieved data.

Together, these two functionalities help overcome major flaws present in traditional LLMs and provide the capability to generate grounded, precise, and context-aware answers.

Key Components of RAG-Based LLMs

1. Retriever Module

The retriever searches for the best external knowledge base to retrieve the most relevant documents or pieces of information.

It employs algorithms like:

- **Dense Passage Retrieval (DPR):** This is a deep learning-based method of semantic search.
- **FAISS (Facebook AI Similarity Search):** It is a library of efficient similarity searches in high-dimensional space.

2. Generator Module

LLM takes both the user query and the retrieved context together to generate the response.

A common generator model is:

- GPT is for natural language understanding and generation.

- T5 (Text-to-Text Transfer Transformer): A General Model for Text Tasks.

3. Knowledge Base

The external source of data, which might be:

- Structured datasets (for example, databases, APIs).
- Data is unstructured (in this case, documents, articles, or research papers).
- A set of real-time data sources, like live web scraping or APIs.

Workflow of RAG-Based LLMs

1. User Query

A user comes up with a question, something like: "What are the health benefits of consuming green tea?"

2. Retrieve

The retriever scans the knowledge base for documents relevant to the question, which may include scientific research or health articles about green tea.

3. Augmented Generation

The generator merges the query with the retrieved documents to create a well-informed, factually based

response:

"Green tea contains antioxidants like catechins that improve brain function and reduce the risk of cardiovascular diseases."

Benefits of RAG-Based LLMs

1. Lower Hallucination

Traditional LLMs tend to produce false or "hallucinated" information. This is because RAG models back their responses with retrieved data and, therefore, tend to have more reliable outputs.

2. Domain Adaptability

RAG models can tap into specific knowledge bases, and this suits applications such as healthcare, legal, and financial services.

3. Timeliness

RAG models avoid the problem of static training data, which may be outdated over time because they will retrieve real-time information.

4. Improved Explainability

The retrieval component enables users to track the source of generated content, thereby promoting trust and transparency.

My Insight:

"RAG-based LLMs address the inherent limitations of large language models, such as outdated knowledge and hallucinations. This hybrid approach ensures more accurate, grounded, and user-centric outputs."

Evaluating RAG-Based LLMs Using the RAGAS Framework

RAG-based LLMs are beneficial, but the retrieval, generator, and knowledge base interact with each other, meaning that their performance is based on all these interactions. Thus, evaluating such systems needs to be structured and comprehensive in order to consider all components. The RAGAS Framework provides an all-encompassing method of evaluation across five dimensions: Retrieval, Accuracy, Generation, Alignment, and Scalability.

What Is the RAGAS Framework?

The RAGAS Framework measures RAG-based LLMs against key performance indicators that are both technically and user-centric. This framework ensures the models are robust, reliable, and appropriate for their applications.

Elements of the RAGAS Framework

1. Retrieval (R)

Focus: Determine the retriever's capability to retrieve relevant, accurate, and timely information from the knowledge base.

Key Metrics:

- Recall: The percentage of all relevant documents retrieved.
- Precision: The proportion of relevant documents that were retrieved.
- Latency: The time needed to access a document.

Evaluations Measures:

- Employ standard datasets for results verification against returned documents.
- The semantic meaning of the query input and the output will be assessed.
- Application in healthcare RAG system; say a search query in "heart diseases" returns irreverent documents relating to lung cancer- poor precision on retrieval.

2. Accuracy (A)

Focus: A measure for ensuring the veracity and correctness of generated output that relies upon LLM.

Key Metrics:

- Factual Consistency: To what extent the output generated agrees with the returned documents.
- Error Rate: Count of incorrect or misleading information

Evaluation Methods:

- Compare the output generated with the ground truth or expert-validated answer.
- Use tools like TruthfulQA for automated fact-checking.
- Example: For an application in finance, for example, a RAG model should depict the retrieved market trends reflected in its reports.

3. Generation (G)

Focus: Measures the quality of the generated text, including fluency, coherence, and relevance.

Key Metrics:

- Coherence: Logical flow of the response.
- Readability: Ease of understanding for the target audience.
- Contextual Relevance: Alignment with the user query.

Evaluation Techniques:

- Human evaluation to rate fluency and coherence.
- Automated metrics, such as BLEU and ROUGE for text quality analysis.
- Example: For a customer support chatbot, responses should be grammatically correct and directly address the customer's concerns.

4. Alignment (A)

Focus: The model should align with user intent, ethical guidelines, and domain-specific requirements.

Key Metrics:

- Intent Alignment: How well the response matches the intent of the user's query.
- Ethical Compliance: Avoidance of biased, harmful, or unethical content.

Evaluation Techniques:

- Use tools such as AI Fairness 360 to detect biases in outputs
- Carry out user satisfaction surveys to measure intent alignment.

- Example: In legal applications, responses should not make unverified legal claims that may mislead users.

5. Scalability (S)

Focus: The model's ability to handle high loads, large datasets, and diverse queries without performance degradation.

Important Measurements

- Latency at Load: Time taken to respond with concurrent usage.
- Throughput: Quantity of queries that are completed within a second.
- Resource Use Efficiency: Utilization of the CPU, GPU, and memory.

Testing Methods

- Simulate high concurrency stress.
- Test on different hardware
- Example: In a holiday sale, an e-commerce product recommendation needs to handle millions of requests with minimal latency.

Practical Application of RAGAS: A Case Study

Project Context

My group built an RAG-based LLM for a healthcare provider. The system produced personalised treatment plans for patients based on their medical history and recent research articles.

Evaluation Using RAGAS

1. Retrieval (R)

Scenario: A retriever accessed a peer-reviewed database of medical journals.

Results:

- Recall: 94% of relevant articles retrieved.
- Precision: 87% of the retrieved documents were directly relevant.
- Latency: Average retrieval time was 200ms.

2. Accuracy (A)

Scenario: Generated treatment plans were reviewed by medical experts.

Results:

- Factual Consistency: 97% match with expert-approved guidelines.
- Error Rate: Only 2 out of 100 outputs had factual errors.

3. Generation (G)

Scenario: Doctors assessed the coherence and readability of the produced reports.

Results:

- Coherence: Scored 4.8/5 on logical flow.
- Readability: 95% of doctors found the outputs readable.

4. Alignment (A)

Scenario: The system was tested for ethical compliance in treatment suggestions.

Results:

- Intent Matching: 98% match with patient-specific queries.
- Ethical Compliance: No harmful or biased recommendations were reported.

5. Scalability (S)

Scenario: Stress tests simulated thousands of concurrent queries.

Results:

- Latency Under Load: Peaked at 250ms, within acceptable limits.
- Throughput: Successfully processed 1,200 queries per second.

Lessons Learned and Improvements

Using the RAGAS Framework, the team identified opportunities to improve retrieval latency and increase precision. By optimising the retriever's indexing strategy and enhancing the generator's context-handling capabilities, overall performance improved by 15%.

RAG-based LLMs are revolutionising the AI landscape by integrating retrieval and generation into a single powerful framework. However, their effectiveness depends on careful evaluation and optimisation. The RAGAS Framework provides a structured, comprehensive approach to assess these systems across critical dimensions, ensuring they deliver accurate, ethical, and scalable results.

This example highlights the importance of RAG-based systems in real-world applications, ranging from healthcare to finance. With the advancement of AI technologies, frameworks like RAGAS will be crucial to make them reliable, usable, and trustworthy.

Chapter 10: Advanced Testing Strategies for New AI Innovation

While AI is rapidly advancing, applications are spreading into diverse fields-from generative AI models such as ChatGPT and DALL·E to autonomous systems such as self-driving cars and warehouse robotics. Such innovation carries transformative potential but brings challenging problems in testing, evaluation, and quality assurance (QA). Advanced testing strategies are needed to ensure such systems are safe, trustworthy, coherent, and reliable in real-world applications.

This chapter explores advanced testing methodologies for generative AI and autonomous systems, discusses future trends in AI testing, and offers insights drawn from my extensive experience in the field to help QA professionals stay updated in this ever-changing domain.

Testing Generative AI Models

The Generative AI models are developed with the capability to generate text, images, audio, and code. Power models come with their uniqueness on challenges such as hallucination, incoherence and a lack of interpretability. It necessitates the testing of such models using strategies designed for different behaviour and use cases by models.

Testing Challenges of Generative AI Models

1. Hallucinations

Hallucination is a phenomenon in which generative models often produce fabricated or nonsensical outputs. For instance, a text-based model could confidently state incorrect facts or provide irrelevant information.

2. Coherence Issues

The outputs should be logically consistent and contextually relevant. For example, a chatbot responding to customer queries must maintain context across multiple turns.

3. Interpretability

Generative AI models are complex and often function as "black boxes," which makes it difficult to explain or trace how specific outputs are generated.

Ethical Concerns

These models may generate biased, harmful, or offensive content if not properly monitored and tested.

Testing Strategies for Generative AI Models

1. Hallucination Testing

- Objective: Detect and minimise fabricated or inaccurate outputs.
- Methods:
    - Compare generated outputs with trusted reference datasets or authoritative sources.
    - Apply automated fact-checking tools, like TruthfulQA, to test for factual coherence.
    - Apply adversarial testing by giving the model ambiguous or misleading queries to test its ability not to hallucinate.
    - For example, a finance-specific generative model hallucinated stock predictions. My team mitigated this by integrating a retrieval-augmented system that grounds the model's outputs in verified financial data.

2. Coherence Testing

- Objective: Test for logical flow and contextual relevance of generated content.
- Methods:
    - Metric evaluation for similarity and coherence in texts using BLEU, ROUGE, etc.
    - Pragmatic testing by simulating realistic usage scenarios. In the case of a virtual assistant, how it would answer multi-turn questions for a wide topic coverage is tested.

- Rating coherence, relevance, and fluency by human evaluators.
- For instance, a chatbot AI could not maintain context while answering a series of questions. The testing team resolved this by improving the memory component of the model to keep track of the conversation history correctly.

3. Interpretability Testing

- Objective: Enhance the transparency and explainability of generative outputs.
- Methods
    - Use tools such as SHAP and LIME to explain model outputs by attributing them to specific inputs or features.
    - Perform counterfactual testing where one provides inputs with slight variations in output change.
    - Create source attribution logs, where the model cites sources or links to materials justifying its response.
    - Explanation: My team applied the technique of interpretability testing for legal text generation. Users will now be able to backtrack any output to the related original legal documents.

4. Bias and Ethical Testing

- Objective: Identify and minimise or mitigate the bias or undesirable acts exhibited by the model results
- Methods

- Use specially designed datasets for probing to identify bias (for example, gender or race).
- Use guidelines and techniques such as red-teaming to test the likelihood of outputs that could cause harm.
- Create feedback loops by using flagged outputs to improve the model.
- Example: A generative chatbot exhibited gender biases in questions related to careers. Through the addition of balanced examples to the training dataset, the team decreased bias by a significant amount.

Testing in Autonomous Systems

Autonomous systems, such as drones, robotic assistants, and self-driving vehicles, work in dynamic and often unpredictable environments. Testing these systems calls for strategies that are safety-centered, reliable, and trustworthy.

Challenges in Testing Autonomous Systems

1. Safety Concerns

The autonomous system must work safely under all conditions, from sensor failures to extreme weather.

2. Trustworthiness

Users must have confidence in the system's ability to make ethical and predictable decisions, especially in applications like healthcare or transportation, where stakes are high.

Complex Interactions

It is expected that such systems face the complexity of multiple-variable interaction, such as with other systems, humans, or environments.

3. Adaptability

Without performance degradation, autonomous systems need to adapt to changing conditions over time.

Testing Strategies of Autonomous Systems

1. Safety Testing

The intent of safety testing is for a system to be safe for use while doing no harm to the environment and the user.

Testing strategies:

- Extremely critical scenarios are simulated, such as sudden obstacles, sensor malfunctions, etc., to test how the system reacts.

- Digital twins (virtual replicas of the physical systems) are used to test high-risk scenarios in a controlled environment.
- HIL testing is conducted to assess the integration of software and physical components.
- Example: A QA team tested a warehouse robot for safety through the simulation of power outages in crowded aisles to ensure that the robot could safely avoid collisions.

2. Reliability Testing

Goal: Demonstrate that the system consistently operates in changing conditions

Methods:

- Perform endurance tests to assess long-term performance.
- Test across environments (for example, changing lighting, temperature, or terrains).
- Introduce controlled failures and measure the fault tolerance recovery mechanisms of the system.
- Example: The reliability of a drone system was tested in high-altitude environments. The team determined altitude-related GPS errors and reconfigured the navigation algorithm to improve reliability.

3. Trustworthiness and Ethical Testing

Objective: Build trust that the system acts ethically and predictably.

Techniques:

- Bias testing needs to be conducted so that the decisions taken by the system are fair and unbiased.

- Test for user interface clarity and transparency so that the users can understand what the system is doing.
- Carry out real-world pilot testing to gather user feedback and evolve the system.

Evolving Trends of AI Testing

AI testing is continuously evolving in complexity. With new challenges, new trends and best practices appear to overcome such difficulties.

1. Testing for Federated Learning

Federated learning is the training of models across decentralised devices, but it also keeps data private. The approach will require strategies for the evaluation of consistency, performance, and security across distributed nodes.

2. Real-Time Monitoring and Adaptive Testing

Continuous monitoring of performance and adaptive feedback loops will be critical for the sustained performance of AI systems within ever-changing environments.

3. Ethical Framework of Testing

With growing concerns about AI ethics, testing frameworks will focus on fairness, accountability, and transparency. Regulatory compliance will play a larger role in development.

4. AI-Assisted Testing

AI will enhance testing processes, including automated bug detection, anomaly detection, and predictive analysis of failures.

5. Digital Twins in Testing

The use of digital twins for simulating real-world scenarios will grow, enabling testers to test AI systems in controlled yet realistic conditions.

Best Practices for Advanced AI Testing

1. Layer-Based Approach

Test every layer, from data preprocessing to the last user interaction.

2. Diverse Datasets

Use diverse and representative datasets to discover biases and for robustness.

3. Cross-disciplinary Collaboration

Involve data scientists, engineers, ethicists, and experts in the domain in your testing.

4. Human-in-the-Loop Testing

Leverage human testers for coherence evaluation tasks, ethical reviews, or scenario-based testing.

5. Record Everything

Maintain clear documentation of testing protocols, results, and model limitations to ensure accountability.

My Tips to Beat the AI Testing Trends

My vast experience in QA arms him with practical insights for professionals navigating the complexities of AI testing.

Here are my tips:

1. Master the Fundamentals of AI and ML

Know the Machine Learning Fundamentals: Algorithms, Data Pipelines, Evaluation Metrics

2. Stay Updated on Tools

Stay updated on tools like Evidently AI, SHAP, Prometheus, and Grafana, which will ease monitoring and testing workflows.

3. Cross-Disciplinary Skills

Combine knowledge of technology with domain experience to precisely address challenges arising in health care, finance, or the retail industries

4. Ethics and Fairness

Anticipate and correct the biases in your systems such that your systems are sound in terms of ethics.

5. Growth Mindset

Maintain curiosity and open up to learn about the newer and latest trends in AI technologies and testing practices.

6. Network and Collaborate

Exchange experiences and insights from the QA and AI communities through various forums, webinars, and conferences.

My Reflection:

"AI testing is not error catching; it's creating a technology that users can rely on. Agile and innovative QA professionals are the ones who will lead this change."

Advanced testing strategies to develop AI innovations- from generative models to autonomous systems are needed because of the unique challenges they present. These strategies range from hallucination testing and coherence evaluation to simulations that aim to test for the safety of an AI system.

While sticking to and tracking current emerging trends and best practices ensures the safest, most reliable, and ethically responsible implementation of AI technologies, I want to end this chapter with a quote I live by:

"One just needs the right mindset and the right set of tools to make impactful changes in AI testing, which is growing dynamically and is challenging at the same time."

Chapter 11: Conclusion and Rahul's Final Thoughts

The journey through the world of AI testing has taken us across complex landscapes filled with challenges and innovative solutions. From understanding the foundational principles of machine learning (ML) testing to exploring advanced techniques for generative AI and autonomous systems, it is evident that the role of quality assurance (QA) in AI is indispensable. It has become very much a necessity to recall and summarise the major testing strategies discussed in this book journey as we are reaching the end of this book. It is also imperative to provide an inspiring message for QA engineers going ahead with their career paths. Besides, we must look forward optimistically toward emerging opportunities and challenges that are going to occur in the fast-paced arena of AI testing in the near future.

This chapter reflects on the valuable insights provided by the author and presents a forward-looking vision of the transformative and pivotal role Quality Assurance is set to play in developing and ensuring the reliability of AI systems.

Summary of Key Testing Strategies

The world of AI is diverse, and so are the testing methodologies that must be followed to ensure that models are accurate, reliable, and ethical. Let's revisit the critical testing strategies discussed throughout this book.

1. Validation Testing

Validation testing serves as the foundation for ensuring that a model meets its performance benchmarks before deployment. It involves:

- Cross-validation to ensure generalizability.
- Testing for overfitting and underfitting to maintain the right balance between training and real-world performance.
- The data pipeline should be run robustly with no anomaly or irregularity that would affect its performance and reliability.

2. Hyperparameter Tuning

Hyperparameter optimization is a critical process that deals with the fine-tuning of many settings, such as the learning rate, the batch size, and the architecture of the complete model in order to provide the highest efficiency and performance for the model. Various techniques, such as grid search and random search are being applied in order to give a systematic and exhaustive inspection of the different hyperparameters in use, which thereafter enhances the overall performance that can be obtained from using the model.

3. Responsible AI Testing

Ensuring that artificial intelligence systems are ethical, fair, and privacy-compliant has emerged as a fundamental cornerstone of quality assurance in this field. The key pillars that support this initiative include:

- Bias detection and mitigation to prevent discrimination.

- Privacy assurance for safeguarding user data and compliance with regulatory standards.
- Evaluating outputs for ethical alignment, especially in generative AI models.

4. Generative AI Testing

Generative models like GPT require unique approaches:

- Hallucination testing to avoid output fabrication.
- Coherence testing to make sure that the answers are logical and relevant to the context.
- Interpretability testing is used to increase the transparency and accountability of the model.

5. Testing of Autonomous Systems

Autonomous systems function in a dynamic environment, requiring testing:

- Safety testing: assessing the behaviour in edge cases and high-risk situations.
- Trustworthiness testing: guaranteeing ethical decision-making and predictable actions.
- Reliability testing: to maintain the consistency of performance in a variety of conditions.

6. Continuous Monitoring

AI models in production require real-time monitoring to detect issues like data drift, prediction errors, or performance degradation.

Automation tools like Prometheus, Evidently AI, and Grafana streamline this process, ensuring long-term reliability.

7. RAGAS Framework

In the world of retrieval-augmented generation (RAG) models, the RAGAS Framework is one of the most complete and structured ways to assess multiple critical factors:

It checks the efficiency of retrieval to retrieve data related and pertinent to tasks. It verifies if the output produced by using the retrieved context is correct or not. It verifies if the decisions are aligned with ethical guidelines and verifies the intent of the user while assessing. The above strategies clearly depict how AI testing is multi-layered and how quality assurance plays a vital role in developing reliable and trustworthy systems.

Motivational message for QA engineers:

QA Engineers Are the Gatekeepers of AI Reliability.

In this vast, evolving AI world, generally QA engineers are working behind the scenes; however, they are revolutionizing work that is just beyond ordinary and remarkable. They are the very foundation architects of trust in the AI world, ensuring with much diligence that various AI systems are implemented to the highest possible standards of accuracy, fairness, and safety in their functionalities. It is very important to realise that without the diligent efforts of QA engineers, even the most advanced and sophisticated AI models would ultimately remain incomplete and unreliable, thereby undermining the integrity of the technology as a whole.

My Message:

"QA in AI is not about debugging alone; it's about ensuring that the systems we build today have a positive impact on the world tomorrow. AI has the power to revolutionise industries, but without your diligence, it can also perpetuate harm. You, as QA engineers, hold the responsibility to ensure AI is ethical, fair, and accessible.".

Remember, in every test you create, each anomaly you catch, and each loophole you meticulously close, the little thing makes a difference in the larger scheme of things. What you do indeed carries so much power because it might protect lives, inspire user trust, and literally form the future trajectory of AI. Whether you are carefully ensuring that a chatbot gives accurate and reliable information or rigorously testing a self-driving car to prevent any possible accidents from occurring, your contributions to this field are absolutely invaluable and cannot be overstated.

QA is not a phase; it is a philosophy. It speaks to excellence and belief in the power of technology that serves humanity responsibly. Feel proud of your role, and never stop pushing for what's possible.

Future of AI in QA: Emerging Opportunities and Challenges Ahead

Emerging Opportunities

1. AI-Powered Testing Tools: As AI matures, QA will benefit from the very technology it tests. AI-driven tools will

- Automate routine work like test case generation and anomaly detection
- Predict model failures through advanced analytics
- Increase the efficiency of testing complex systems, making the QA process faster and reliable

2. AI in Specialized Testing Domains: AI is quickly being adopted in specialist domains, including:

- Healthcare: Testing models for diagnostic accuracy and ethics
- Finance: Testing for fairness and transparency in fraud detection systems.
- Autonomous Vehicles: A Holistic Safety and Reliability Assessment in Real-World Environments. As the market matures, domain-specific QA engineers with years of experience and knowledge in these niche industries will be more highly sought after and in greater demand.

3. Continuous and real-time monitoring: AI models are rarely static by nature and very often require continuous attention and fine-tuning. Real-time monitoring with adaptive testing pipelines will soon become the norm of practice, enabling QA teams to detect and correct performance issues and biases during the production environment, ensuring optimal functionality and fairness all the way through the system life cycle.

4. Explainable AI (XAI) Testing: With increased awareness and momentum about the growing need for transparency in AI, quality assurance will soon have a role to play that is more vital than ever: it will not only have to ensure that the model is interpretable but also that the AI itself can explain the decisions that the model is making. Indeed, this kind of transparency is critical when AI applications have severe stakes, such as in the legal or medical fields, where a slight mistake in the decision will have serious implications for one's life or well-being.

5. Federated Learning: With federated learning, where training models occur across decentralised devices, QA engineers will check consistency, security, and performance in distributed environments.

Challenges Ahead

1. The Increasing Complexity of AI Systems: As the size and ability of models increase, the inner workings of those systems become more difficult to grasp. The QA professional will need advanced tools and instruction to adequately test these complex systems.

2. Dynamic Environments: AI systems run in real-world environments with constantly changing conditions. Testing for adaptability and robustness in such environments will remain a significant challenge.

3. Ethical and Regulatory Pressures: Governments and organizations are imposing increasingly stringent AI regulations. QA teams must ensure compliance with these rules while balancing the ethical considerations in areas like bias, privacy, and accountability.

4. Balancing Speed and Thoroughness: QA professionals need to test models properly without delaying timelines in an industry that has fast deployment cycles - a balancing act requiring both efficiency and precision.

5. Cross-disciplinary collaboration: Teams contributing to an AI system represent multiple domains, such as data science, engineering, ethics, and business. QA engineers need to operate across disciplines; hence, bridging gaps requires high collaboration and communication.

"The Future of AI Is Built on Excellent QA"

Quality assurance has often been overlooked in the development lifecycle. However, it has become one of the most critical foundations for the success of AI systems. In the near future, QA engineers are expected to lead innovation, ethics, and reliability.

My Reflection:

"The challenges are huge, but so are the opportunities. QA professionals are unsung heroes who ensure AI systems don't just work but shine. As AI becomes an integral part of our lives, your role as a QA engineer will only grow in importance."

It is going to be about adaptability, teamwork, and learning. It is going to be all about being curious and embracing change. Always remember that your impact on society matters. Each test you conduct not only enhances a system but also builds trust, ensures safety, and shapes the future of technology..

This is indeed a stimulating and thrilling time to be associated with the field of Quality Assurance, and I am confident that you are better equipped than ever before to face the various challenges and the multitude of opportunities that lie in store for us. Together, let's work towards creating a world where artificial intelligence is not only advanced and intelligent but ethical, fair in its applications, and consistently reliable in its performance.

AI testing is far more than a technical process; it's a responsibility. From detection of biases to ensuring safety in autonomous systems, the QA professional is the one who guards reliability and trust in AI. The book has provided a roadmap for navigating the challenges and embracing opportunities in AI testing, but the journey doesn't end here.

The future trajectory and advancement of artificial intelligence are contingent upon the commitment, intellect, and elevated ethical standards exhibited by quality assurance engineers. With the appropriate tools, a visionary perspective, and a well-defined understanding of the realm of possibilities, one possesses the capacity to influence and speed up the advancement of artificial intelligence toward a more promising future that will ultimately benefit all members of society. As I conclude this book, I want to leave you motivated and thoughtful with this quote:

"The best QA engineers don't just test systems; they inspire trust in technology."

Together, let us rise to the challenge and drive the future forward—one thoughtful, rigorous test at a time—knowing that our work shapes a world where innovation and reliability go hand in hand.

Verses Kindler Publication

Verses Kindler Publication

Reach us through our website -

https://www.verseskindlerpublication.com/

For more information visit our

Instagram or Facebook page.